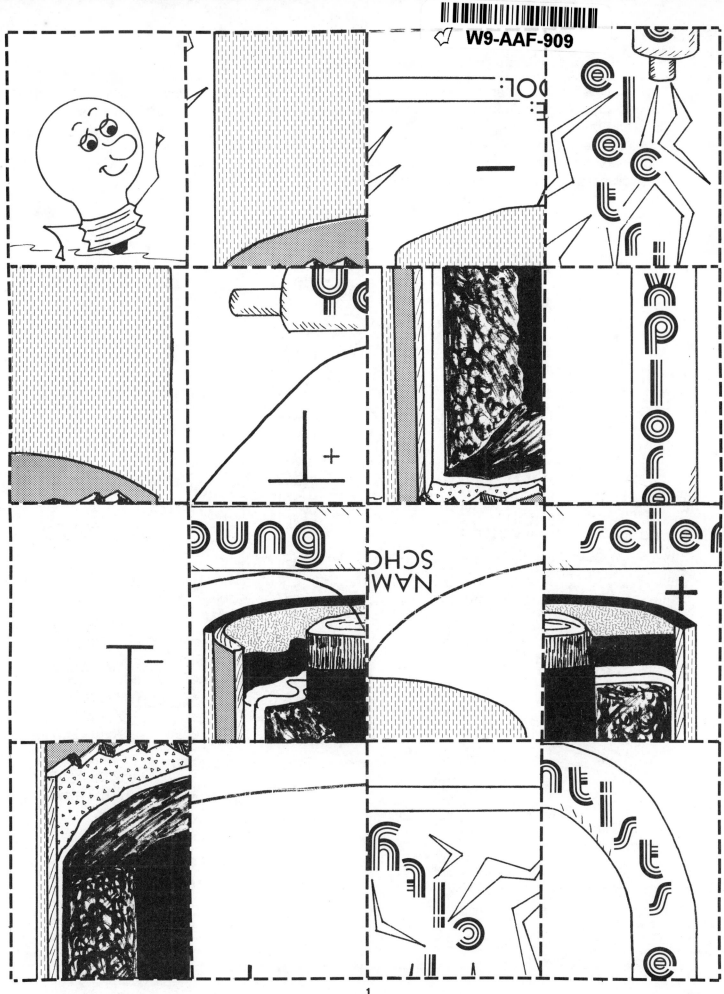

W9-AAF-909

PROCESS SKILL(S): CHECK

ELECTRICITY REFERENCE MATERIALS

Scientists CHECK reference materials to learn about electricity. Below are pages from an encyclopedia and dictionary. Check the encyclopedia pages for information on scientists and their discoveries. Write the number of the scientist on page 2 in the blank next to the correct discovery on page 3. On a sheet of paper, write the terms found on the dictionary pages below in alphabetical order. Define each term. Add more pages to your encyclopedia and dictionary as you learn more about electricity.

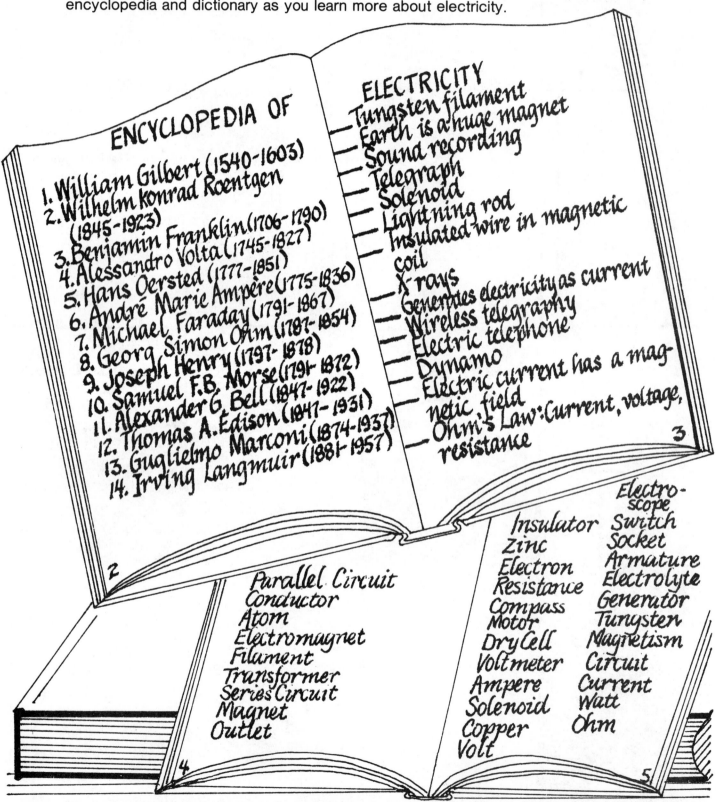

ENCYCLOPEDIA OF

1. William Gilbert (1540-1603)
2. Wilhelm Konrad Roentgen (1845-1923)
3. Benjamin Franklin (1706-1790)
4. Alessandro Volta (1745-1827)
5. Hans Oersted (1777-1851)
6. André Marie Ampère (1775-1836)
7. Michael Faraday (1791-1867)
8. Georg Simon Ohm (1787-1854)
9. Joseph Henry (1797-1878)
10. Samuel F.B. Morse (1791-1872)
11. Alexander G. Bell (1847-1922)
12. Thomas A. Edison (1847-1931)
13. Guglielmo Marconi (1874-1937)
14. Irving Langmuir (1881-1957)

ELECTRICITY
___ Tungsten filament
___ Earth is a huge magnet
___ Sound recording
___ Telegraph
___ Solenoid
___ Lightning rod
___ Insulated wire in magnetic coil
___ X-rays
___ Generates electricity as current
___ Wireless telegraphy
___ Electric telephone
___ Dynamo
___ Electric current has a magnetic field
___ Ohm's Law: Current, voltage, resistance

Parallel Circuit
Conductor
Atom
Electromagnet
Filament
Transformer
Series Circuit
Magnet
Outlet

Insulator
Zinc
Electron
Resistance
Compass
Motor
Dry Cell
Voltmeter
Ampere
Solenoid
Copper
Volt

Electroscope
Switch
Socket
Armature
Electrolyte
Generator
Tungsten
Magnetism
Circuit
Current
Watt
Ohm

2

PROCESS SKILL(S): CHECK

HOME/SCHOOL SAFETY AND MATERIALS CHECK

Scientists do indoor and outdoor electrical safety CHECKS around the home and school. Check (✓) the light bulb if you feel the statement is a wise safety check, (X) if unwise. Then interview an electrician to find out if your results are correct.

Outdoor Electricial Safety

1. Keep kites away from power lines.
2. Keep model airplanes and rockets away from power lines.
3. Use wire on kites instead of string.
4. Fly kite in sunny, not rainy, weather.
5. Do not pull on kite string when it's caught in a power line.
6. Do climb electrical pole if kite is caught in electrical wires.
7. Stay away from electrical boxes and circuit breakers.
8. Leave electrical relay substations alone.
9. Do touch fallen electrical wires.
10. Stay in car if power line falls on car.
11. Do not play outside when it's raining.
12. Do swim in rainy weather.
13. Do not light a flame over a car battery.
14. Look for UL label on all electrical devices you and your parents buy.

Indoor Electrical Safety

1. Do not touch electric cord while standing in or near water.
2. Do have radio on or near bathtub.
3. Tape or get rid of worn electrical cords.
4. Use a fire extinguisher rated for electrical fires, not water filled extinguisher or water, to extinguish electrical fire.
5. Pull electrical plug out by plug, not cord.
6. Unplug appliances before fixing.
7. Do not place too many plugs in one electrical outlet.
8. Have three-prong grounded tools or tools that are double insulated.
9. Do not touch appliances with wet hands.
10. Do stick bare electrical wires into electrical outlets.
11. Use electrical toys and appliances with care.
12. Keep electrical cords where people won't trip over them.
13. Replace a fuse by using a penny in fuse box.
14. Hide electrical wires under rugs or carpets.

MATERIALS CHECK: You, as a scientist, will need these materials for your study of electricity and magnetism in this book. Check (✓) the box as you gather each item.

☐ Dictionary	☐ Thumbtacks	☐ Burned Out Light Bulb
☐ Paper Clips	☐ Tape	☐ Magnet
☐ Encyclopedia	☐ Cardboard	☐ Flashlight
☐ Paper Fasteners	☐ Plastic Film Can Top	☐ 1 Dead Carbon Dry Cell
☐ Scissors	☐ Shoe Box	☐ 1 3v Flashlight Bulb
☐ Glue	☐ Paper Bag	☐ No. 22 Insulated Copper Wire
☐ Pencil	☐ 2 Empty Ball-Point Pens	☐ Other_____
☐ Ruler	☐ Other_____	☐ Other_____

SECRET SYMBOLS CONCENTRATION

To be a scientist you must THINK ABOUT and REMEMBER many things. Scientists often THINK about and REMEMBER an object by drawing a symbol which is a picture of something that stands for the object.

Cut apart the six electrical symbol cards (A-F) below. Make card deck. Cut apart six electrical object cards (G-L) that match the electrical symbols. Make card deck of these. Glue each card to stiff cardboard. Using the words below, identify each object and its symbol by writing its name under the picture on the card. Match symbol card to object card. Play Concentration with your friends. Use these words to write on cards: dry cell, ground, bulb, fuse, switch, connected wires.

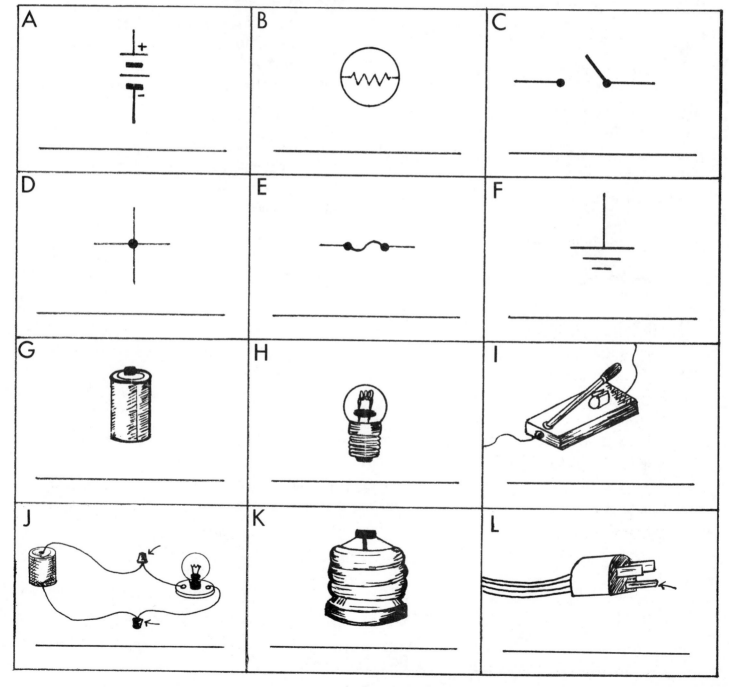

PROCESS SKILL(S): THINK, REMEMBER

SECRET SYMBOLS AROUND HOME

Below is an inside view of a house that includes electrical objects and their names which you can THINK about and REMEMER. In the box next to the name of each object, draw the correct symbol that best matches that object. Choose from the symbols listed below. On the other side of this page, make a list of electrical objects and their symbols found around your home. Find the meaning of the *UL* symbol printed on the tag of the iron cord. Print the symbol *UL* after each appliance in your home that has a *UL* symbol.

1. DRY CELLS
2. FUSE BOX
3. PLUG WIRES
4. IRON TAG
5. SWITCH
6. MICROWAVE CORD
7. BULB

SYMBOLS TO CHOOSE FROM:

UL

5

WHAT'S INSIDE THE BLACK BOX?

Young scientists ask QUESTIONS about things in the world around them. Here is a drawing of a black box and lighted light bulb.

What do you think is inside the black box causing the bulb to light? Mark an **X** in the box under each drawing below if you think the object inside the box causes the bulb to light.

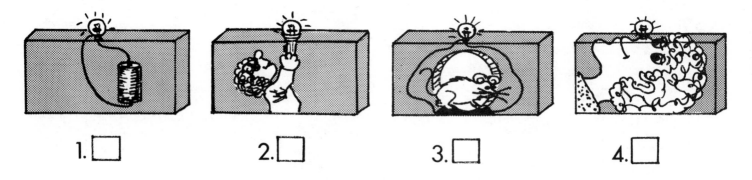

1. ☐   2. ☐   3. ☐   4. ☐

In the box below, make a drawing of what you think is inside the black box causing the bulb to light. Then create your own black box with lighted light bulb to show your friends.

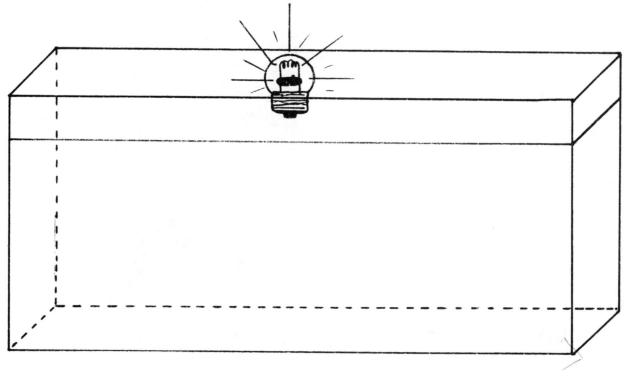

6

PROCESS SKILL(S): QUESTION

WHAT'S INSIDE A FLASHLIGHT?

Scientists often ask the QUESTION, "What objects are needed to make a flashlight work?" Below is a picture of a flashlight that has missing parts. Observe and name each missing part. How does each part make the flashlight light? Cut out and glue each part to the correct location on the flashlight. Write a mystery story about how a flashlight has helped you find a missing object or friend in the dark.

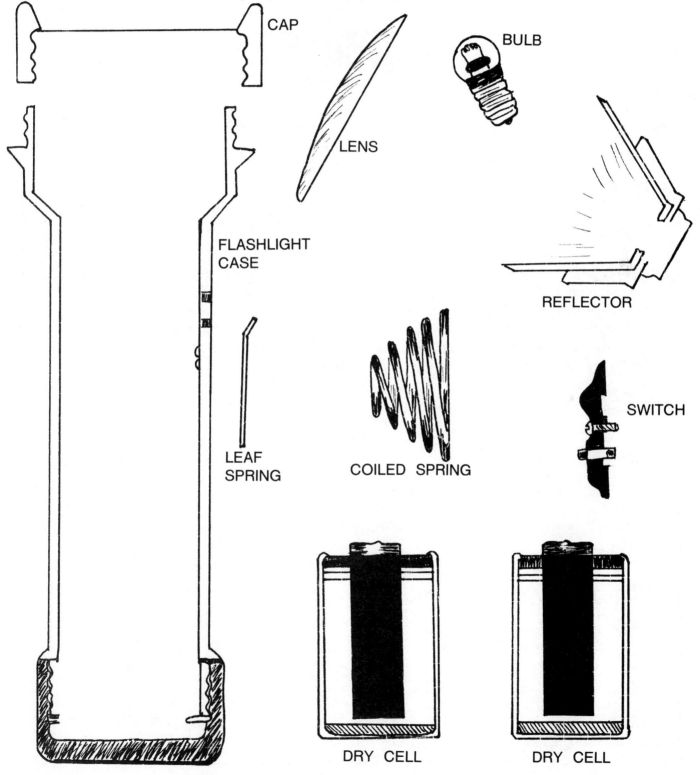

CAP

LENS

BULB

REFLECTOR

FLASHLIGHT CASE

LEAF SPRING

COILED SPRING

SWITCH

DRY CELL

DRY CELL

7

PROCESS SKILL(S): OBSERVATION

OBSERVE THE DRY CELL, LIGHT BULB AND . . .

Young scientists OBSERVE carefully to learn how things look and work. Below are pictures of a dry cell, light bulb and scrambled words that identify each part. With help from your teacher, use pliers to take apart a **D** dry cell. **CAUTION**: Do **NOT** take apart alkaline or nickel cadmium dry cells, as they are dangerous. Unscramble the word below each part found. Write its name in the correct blank. On the back of this page, make drawings of the parts of a dry cell.

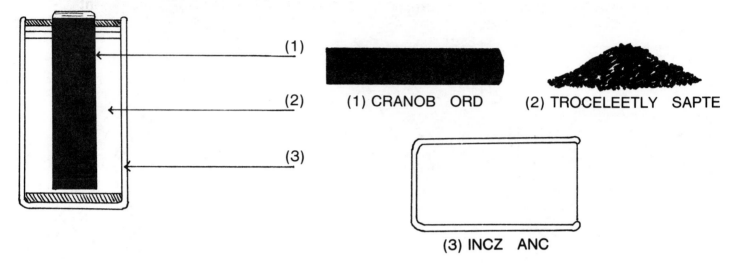

(1) CRANOB ORD

(2) TROCELEETLY SAPTE

(3) INCZ ANC

Below is a picture of a light bulb. With help from your teacher, place burned out light bulb in paper sack. **CAUTION:** Do not use fluorescent bulbs. Gently rap paper sack over table to break bulb. Carefully remove parts of bulb from sack. Observe and identify each part. Unscramble the words below. Write the name of each part in the corresponding blank. In the blanks next to the bulb, write the **numbers** of the correct parts. On the back of this page, make drawings of the parts of a light bulb.

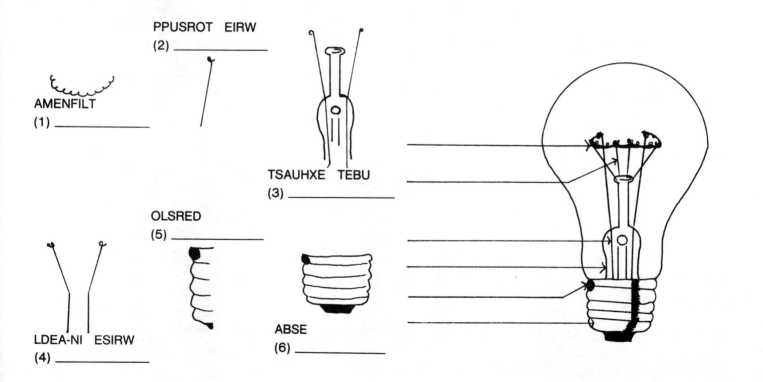

PPUSROT EIRW
(2) _____

AMENFILT
(1) _____

TSAUHXE TEBU
(3) _____

OLSRED
(5) _____

LDEA-NI ESIRW
(4) _____

ABSE
(6) _____

8

FLASHLIGHT

Observe the flashlight below. It is like the one you put together on page 7. With help from your teacher or parents, take apart, then put together a flashlight. Turn on flashlight. Observe brightness (intensity) of light. Cover end of flashlight with thin sheets of tissue paper until light can no longer be seen. Write the **number** of these sheets on the intensity meter box below. Look up the words **opaque, translucent** and **transparent** in your dictionary. Write the definition of each word in the blanks below.

Scientists sometimes can't observe something directly but they still know that it is there. Such is the case with the flow of electricity in a flashlight. With a pen, connect the arrows on the flashlight below to show the path of electricity. Then make a list of things that you cannot observe with your eyes but you know are there. Write these in your science log.

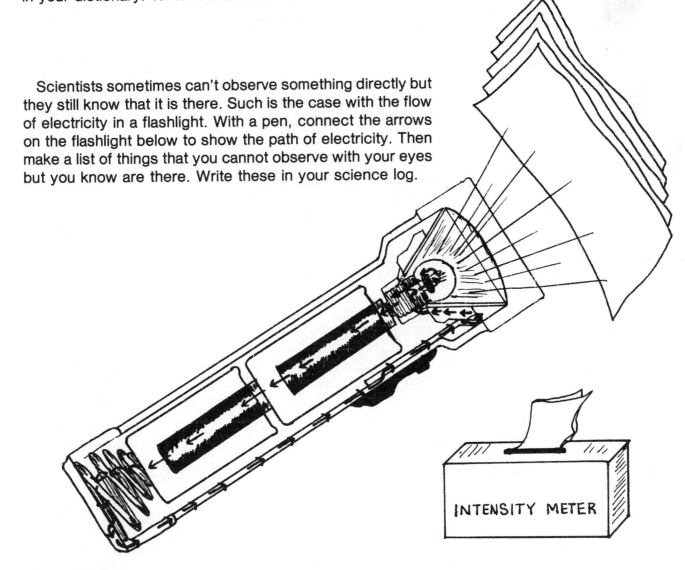

INTENSITY METER

DEFINITIONS:

(1) opaque (ō-pāk') adj. _____

(2) translucent (trăns-lōō'sənt) adj. _____

(3) transparent (trăns-pâr'ənt) adj. _____

QUESTIONS:

(1) What happens when you place one dry cell in the opposite direction in the flashlight?

(2) How does the flip of the switch make the light glow in a flashlight?

LIGHT UP AND...

Scientists PREDICT or guess when or how something might happen. You can do the same. Use dry cells, flashlight bulb and piece of wire to find out if the bulb will or won't light in each drawing below. Guess first by circling *Will light* or *Won't light*. Then try to light the bulb. Circle whether *It lit* or *Didn't light.* Record your total score in the blanks at the bottom of the page. Then try other ways to light the bulb.

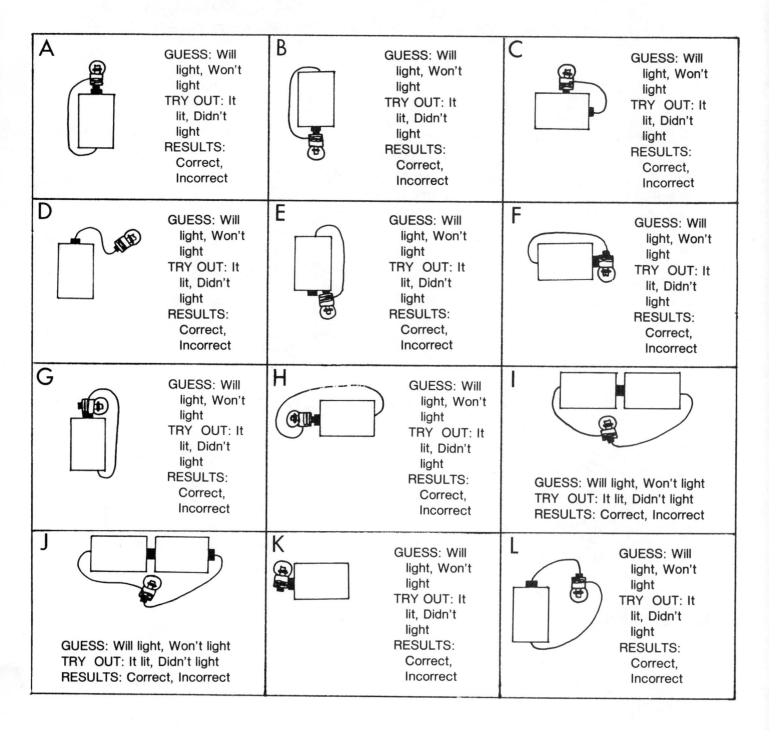

Number Correct_____

Number Incorrect_____

Percent Correct_____

10

ATTRACT!

Two ends of 8 bar magnets below are attracted to two ends of the horseshoe magnet at the top of the page. In each prediction box below, PREDICT then write, the number and letter of the magnet at the bottom of the maze that will be attracted to the correct pole of the magnet at the top of the maze. Then try out your prediction by drawing a line with your pencil to show the correct route. Record answer in answer box. Tell your friends about the attractive force you discovered between magnets. Write a play or story on how the same force could influence people.

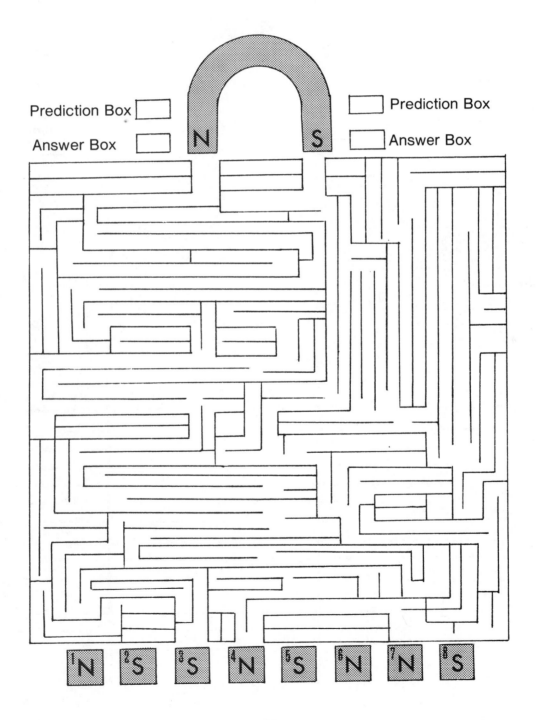

Prediction Box ☐   ☐ Prediction Box

Answer Box ☐   ☐ Answer Box

N   S

N   S   S   N   S   N   N   S

11

PROCESS SKILL(S): CLASSIFY

ATTRACTIVE CLASS!

Objects are classified into groups because they have a similar feature. Some objects may be attracted to a magnet, others may not. Find and circle the 15 listed objects in the classroom picture below. In the My Guess column, place M (magnetic) if you think the object will be attracted to a magnet, NM (nonmagnetic) if it won't be attracted. Then with a magnet, locate and test each listed classroom object. In the chart below, CLASSIFY (✓) each object as magnetic or nonmagnetic based on the results of your tests. On the chalkboard in the picture below, list eight other magnetic objects found in your classroom.

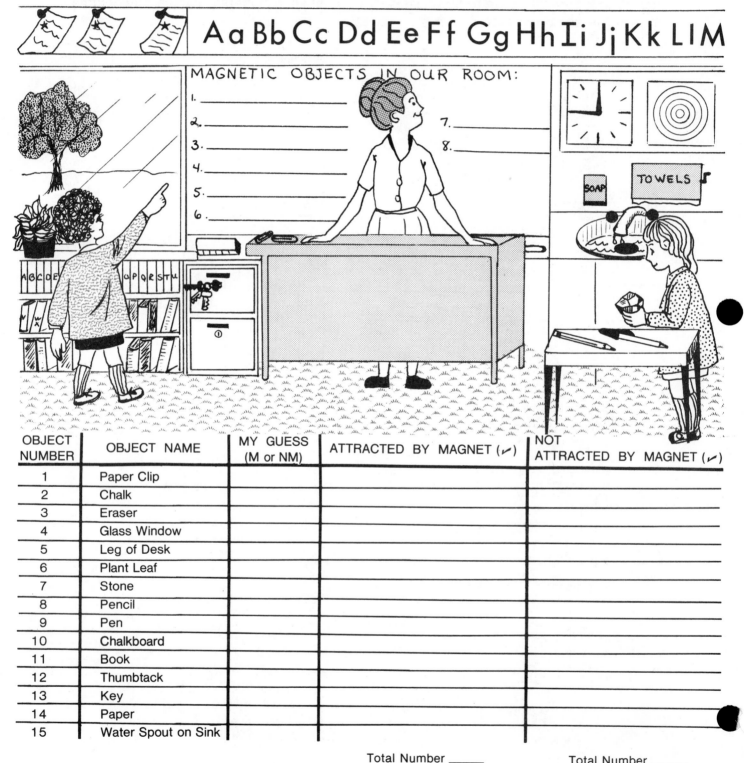

OBJECT NUMBER	OBJECT NAME	MY GUESS (M or NM)	ATTRACTED BY MAGNET (✓)	NOT ATTRACTED BY MAGNET (✓)
1	Paper Clip			
2	Chalk			
3	Eraser			
4	Glass Window			
5	Leg of Desk			
6	Plant Leaf			
7	Stone			
8	Pencil			
9	Pen			
10	Chalkboard			
11	Book			
12	Thumbtack			
13	Key			
14	Paper			
15	Water Spout on Sink			

Total Number _____   Total Number _____

PROCESS SKILL(S): CLASSIFY

ALL ABOARD: CONDUCTOR CLASSIFICATION

Scientists CLASSIFY objects that electricity can or cannot pass through as being conductors or nonconductors (insulators). Build conductor tester shown below. Wind wire around points of thumbtacks and insert into ends of empty ball-point pens or meat skewers. Connect to battery and bulb with holder as shown. With ends of tester, test objects listed in the chart below. Observe whether bulb is bright (good conductor), dim (poor conductor) or didn't light (nonconductor). In the chart, classify (✔) each object as a Good Conductor, Poor Conductor, or Nonconductor.

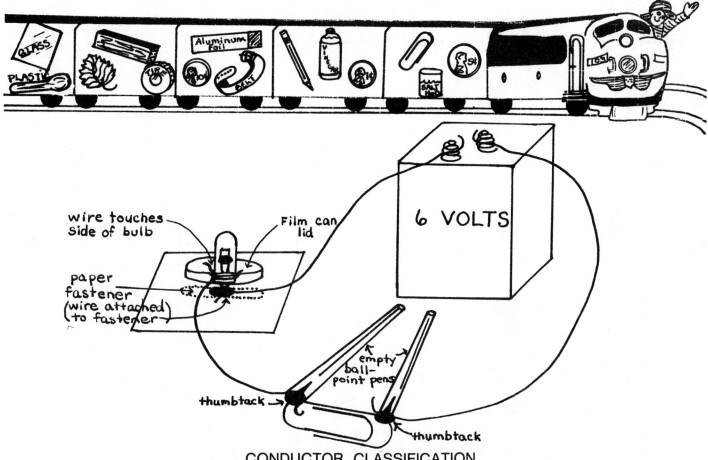

CONDUCTOR CLASSIFICATION

Object	Good Conductor	Poor Conductor	Nonconductor (Insulator)
Paper Clip			
Silver Coin			
5¢ Piece			
Copper Cent			
Lead Pencil			
Aluminum Foil			
Wood			
Glass			
Plant Leaf			
Vinegar			
Leather			
Rubber			
Salt Water			
Plastic			

13

COMPARISONS AT SCHOOL

Scientists COMPARE objects to learn ways in which the objects are or are not alike. COMPARE the drawings below. Circle the word that best describes the picture correctly. Then compare the pictures on this page with those on page 15. How are they alike? How are they different?

1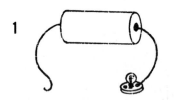

CLOSED OR OPEN CIRCUIT

2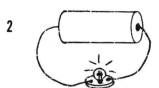

COMPLETE OR SHORT CIRCUIT

3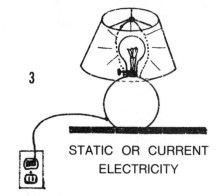

STATIC OR CURRENT ELECTRICITY

4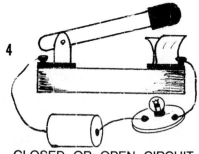

CLOSED OR OPEN CIRCUIT

5

SERIES OR PARALLEL CIRCUIT

6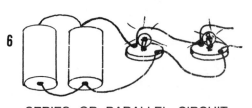

SERIES OR PARALLEL CIRCUIT

7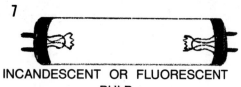

INCANDESCENT OR FLUORESCENT BULB

8

DRY CELL OR WET CELL

9

CONDUCTOR OR INSULATOR

10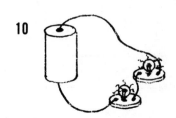

SERIES OR PARALLEL CIRCUIT

11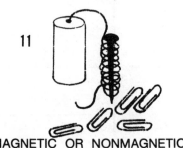

MAGNETIC OR NONMAGNETIC

12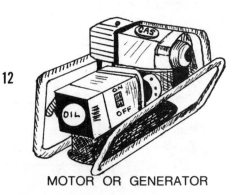

MOTOR OR GENERATOR

PROCESS SKILL(S): COMPARE

COMPARISONS AT HOME

Scientists COMPARE objects to learn ways in which the objects are or are not alike. COMPARE the drawings below. Circle the word that best describes the picture correctly. Then compare these pictures with those on page 14. How are they alike? How are they different?

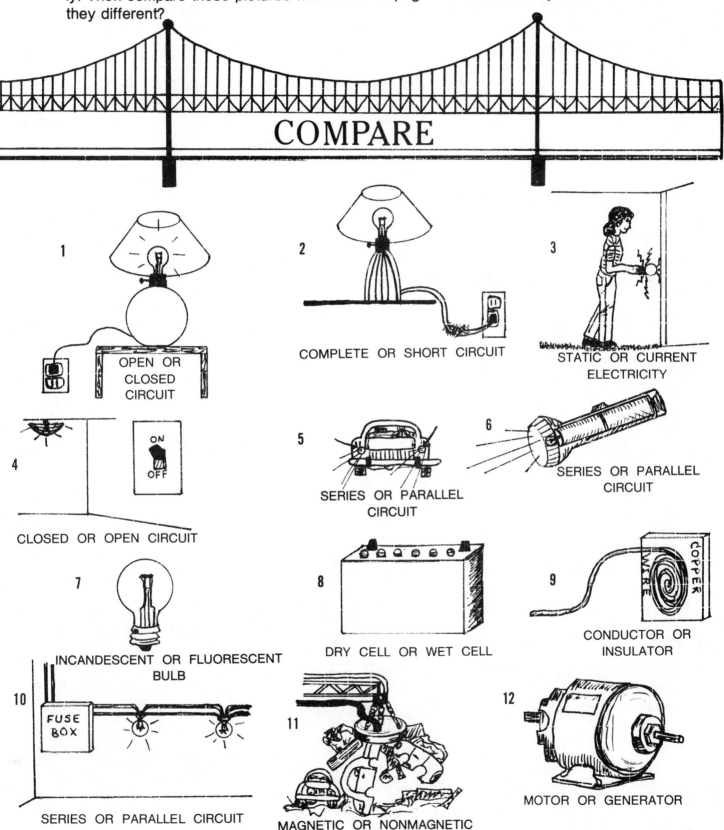

1. OPEN OR CLOSED CIRCUIT

2. COMPLETE OR SHORT CIRCUIT

3. STATIC OR CURRENT ELECTRICITY

4. CLOSED OR OPEN CIRCUIT

5. SERIES OR PARALLEL CIRCUIT

6. SERIES OR PARALLEL CIRCUIT

7. INCANDESCENT OR FLUORESCENT BULB

8. DRY CELL OR WET CELL

9. CONDUCTOR OR INSULATOR

10. SERIES OR PARALLEL CIRCUIT

11. MAGNETIC OR NONMAGNETIC

12. MOTOR OR GENERATOR

15

PROCESS SKILL(S): ESTIMATE

SCHOOL ESTIMATES

Scientists often form an opinion on the number, size or value of something. This opinion is called an ESTIMATE. In the My Estimate column below, write your estimate of the number, size or value of the listed electrical items found in your school or classroom. Find out the number, size or value for each item. Record your results in the Actual column. Then record the difference between your estimate and actual result for each item.

ITEM	MY ESTIMATE	ACTUAL	DIFFERENCE
Last Month's School Electric Bill in Dollars			
Length of Fluorescent Light Bulb			
Number of Computers at School			
Cost of a Tape Recorder			
Length and Width of P.A. System Speaker			
Number of Telephones in School			
Cost of Electric Typewriter			
Length of a Fire Extinguisher			
Number of Electric Clocks in School			
Cost of 16mm Projector			
Length and Width of Electronic Calculator			
Number of Volts Required to Run a Slide Projector			
Cost of an Electronic Game			
Diameter of Burner on a Hot Plate or Stove			
Number of Receptacles with Two Blades and Ground Slot in Your Classroom			
Cost of an Electric Pencil Sharpener			
Length of Electrical Cord on Overhead Projector			
Number of Electrical Switches in Your Classroom			

HOME ESTIMATES

Scientists often form an opinion on the number, size or value of something. This opinion is called an ESTIMATE. In the My Estimate column below, write your estimate of the number, size or value of the home electrical items listed below . Find out the number, size or value for each item. Record your results in the Actual column. Then record the difference between your estimate and actual result for each item.

ITEM	MY ESTIMATE	ACTUAL	DIFFERENCE
Last Month's Home Electric Bill in Dollars	_____	_____	_____
Length of Electrical Cord on Toaster	_____	_____	_____
Number of Electric Motors in the Home	_____	_____	_____
Initial Cost of Buying an Electric Radio	_____	_____	_____
Length and Width of Electrical Wall Switch Plate	_____	_____	_____
Number of Incandescent Light Bulbs in the Home	_____	_____	_____
Initial Cost of Buying a Hair Dryer	_____	_____	_____
Length of Extended Rabbit Ear TV Antenna	_____	_____	_____
Number of Electrical Switches in the Home	_____	_____	_____
Initial Cost of Buying an Electric Range	_____	_____	_____
Distance Around the Base of Incandescent Light Bulb	_____	_____	_____
Number of Dials on Electric Meter at Home	_____	_____	_____
Initial Cost of Buying a Computer for the Home	_____	_____	_____
Length of Electrical Cord on Vacuum Cleaner	_____	_____	_____
Number of Volts Required to Run a Refrigerator	_____	_____	_____
Cost of Electric Wheelchair	_____	_____	_____
Length of Fluorescent Light Bulb	_____	_____	_____
Number of Amps Required to Run an Electric Iron	_____	_____	_____

MEASURE UP AND...

Scientists often need to MEASURE various lengths of electrical wire in their work. Help the scientist plan to wire the house below. With a string and/or ruler, MEASURE the lengths of wire needed to connect various points listed in the chart below. Record these measurements in the columns on the chart. The first one is done for you. You will need these measurements to trace the paths of wire that form electrical circuits in the house on page 19.

				Length of Wire Needed	
From This Point	Object	To This Point	Object	Inches	Cm
A	Transformer Pole	B	Electric Meter	4.0	10.0
B	Electric Meter	C	Fuse Box		
C	Fuse Box	D	Refrigerator		
C	Fuse Box	E	Light in Kitchen		
C	Fuse Box	F	Attic Fan		
C	Fuse Box	G	Outlet in Kitchen		
H	Switch in Kitchen	E	Light in Kitchen		
C	Fuse Box	I	Light in Basement		
C	Fuse Box	J	Outlet in Basement		
C	Fuse Box	K	Television		
C	Fuse Box	L	Outlet in Bedroom		
C	Fuse Box	M	Washer		

WIRE UP

Lines drawn between each pair of letters below are wires needed to connect electrical objects in the house. With a ruler, MEASURE the length of each wire. Record length in inches (cm) on each wire. Using a different colored pen for each wire, trace the wire that connects two lettered points to form a circuit in the house. The first one, point A (transformer) to point B (electric meter) 4.0 inches (10.0 cm), is done for you. Trace remaining circuits. Identify electrical objects found on each circuit. Then write a story about the route you would take if you were electricity that travels throughout your home.

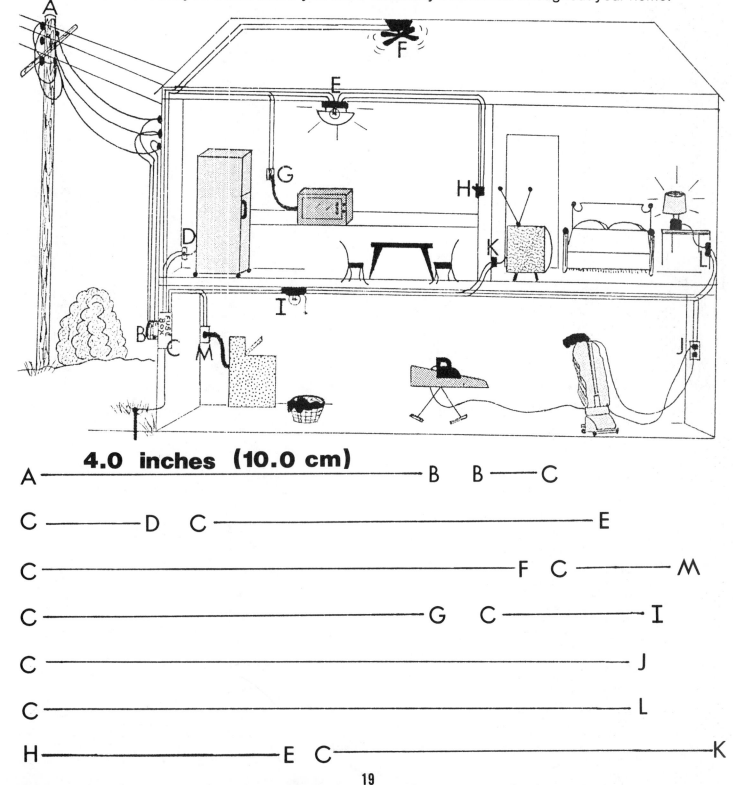

4.0 inches (10.0 cm)

A ————————————————— B   B ——— C

C ——— D   C —————————————— E

C —————————————— F   C ——— M

C —————————————— G   C ——— I

C —————————————— J

C —————————————— L

H ———————— E   C —————————————— K

19

HELP FIND AC AND DC

In the picture below, find and **circle** all the objects that operate on dry cell (DC—direct current) electricity. Draw a **square** around all the objects that require an electrical current (AC—alternating current). In the BAR GRAPHS below, color in one box for each object found. Write the name of the object in the blank next to the box. Count both the number of circled and squared objects. Place these numbers in the square and circle marked *total* below.

Show your results to your friends, teachers and parents. On the other side of this page, make a list of all electrical objects and the type of electricity they use in your home or school.

Name of Object

Name of Object

Total

Total

PROCESS SKILL(S): GRAPHING

MY BOOK OF HOME ELECTRICITY USE

Scientists make LINE GRAPHS to help them understand how much electricity appliances use. Below are sample pages of a book that will help you record electrical use in your home. With help from your parents, read electric meter each day. Draw arrows in proper places on dials below. Subtract yesterday's reading from today's reading to find daily usage in kilowatt hours. Then make a line graph below that shows each day's electrical consumption.

MY BOOK OF HOME

ELECTRICITY USE

Name ______________________

School ______________________

Today's Reading ______________________kWh

Yesterday's Reading ______________________kWh

Total kWh Used ______________________

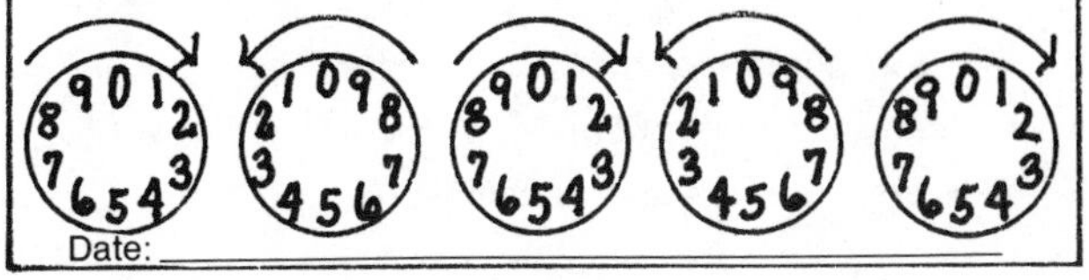

Date: ______________________

Today's Reading ______________________kWh

Yesterday's Reading ______________________kWh

Total kWh Used ______________________

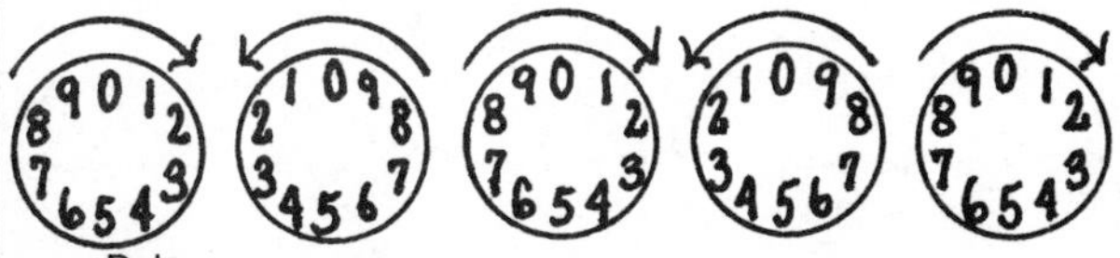

Date: ______________________

Today's Reading ______________________kWh

Yesterday's Reading ______________________kWh

Total kWh Used ______________________

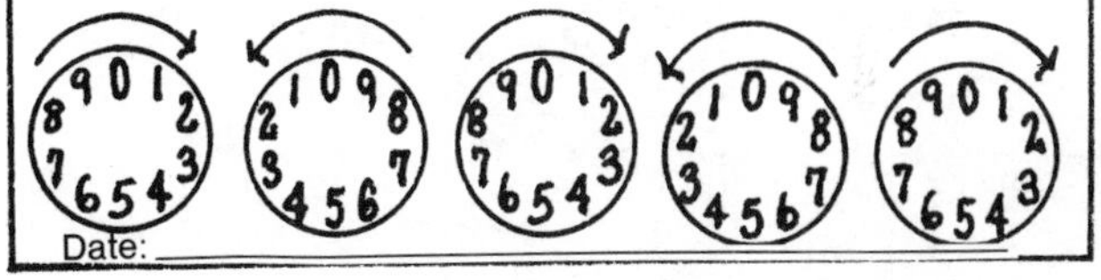

Date: ______________________

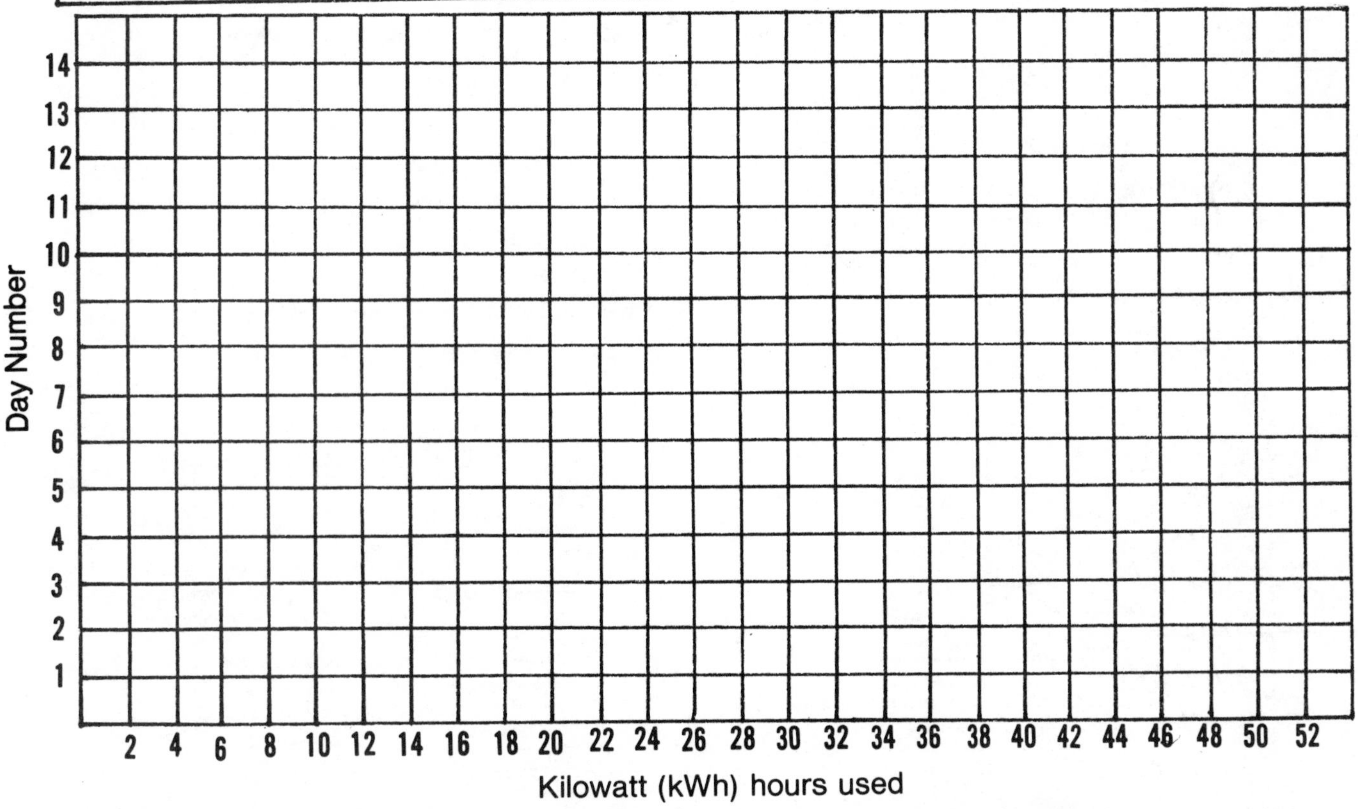
Day Number
1 2 3 4 5 6 7 8 9 10 11 12 13 14
2 4 6 8 10 12 14 16 18 20 22 24 26 28 30 32 34 36 38 40 42 44 46 48 50 52
Kilowatt (kWh) hours used

CHALLENGE ACTIVITY: Acquire past monthly bills of electrical consumption from your parents. Make a line graph to show home electrical consumption for the past twelve months.

PROCESS SKILL(S): TEST

YOUNG SCIENTISTS TEST EQUIPMENT AND . . .

Before scientists begin to experiment, they TEST equipment to make sure it works. Below are pictures of simple electrical gadgets that you can make, then test, to see if they work.

LIGHT BULB HOLDER

Materials: paper fastener, cardboard, wire (2), plastic film can top (free from film processing centers), light bulb, dry cell

Procedure: Punch hole in film can top with pencil. Screw in bulb. Connect one wire from top of dry cell to side of dry cell to side of bulb by sliding wire up through film can top against bulb. Attach another wire to paper fastener and tape to bottom of dry cell. Be sure bulb touches paper fastener to make bulb light.

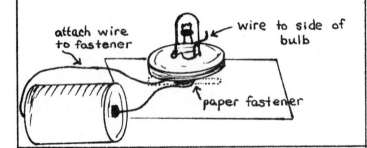

PAPER CLIP SWITCH

Materials: 2 paper fasteners, paper clip, wires, light bulb, dry cell, cardboard, light bulb holder

Procedure: Punch two paper fasteners through cardboard. Attach paper clip and wires to paper fasteners and light bulb in bulb holder as shown below. Slide paper clip switch to make light bulb go on and off.

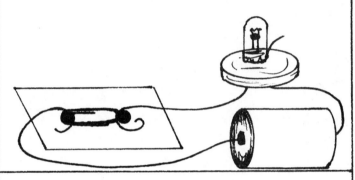

QUIZ GAME

Materials: 16 paper clips, 11 wires, bulb and bulb holder, dry cell, cardboard

Procedure: Attach paper clips and wires to cardboard as shown below. This makes back side of quiz game.

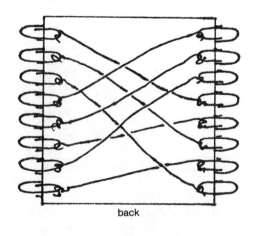

back

QUIZ GAME

Procedure: Assemble dry cell, light bulb and holder with wires as shown below. Cut out page 23 and glue to cardboard. Test your knowledge of electricity. Remember, if you touch two paper clips and the light goes on, you have answered the question correctly. Keep a record of your results.

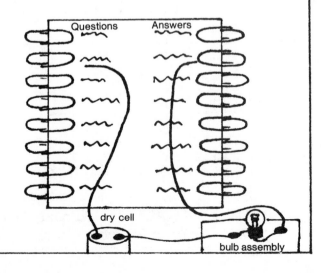

22

PROCESS SKILL(S): TEST

THEIR KNOWLEDGE

Cut out quiz board game below. Glue to piece of cardboard. Connect wires between paper clips on back of cardboard as shown on page 22. Set up dry cell and light bulb. TEST knowledge of electricity by touching wires that complete the circuit between question and corresponding answer. Keep a record of results. Write more questions and answers. Insert on quiz board. Change questions and answers frequently.

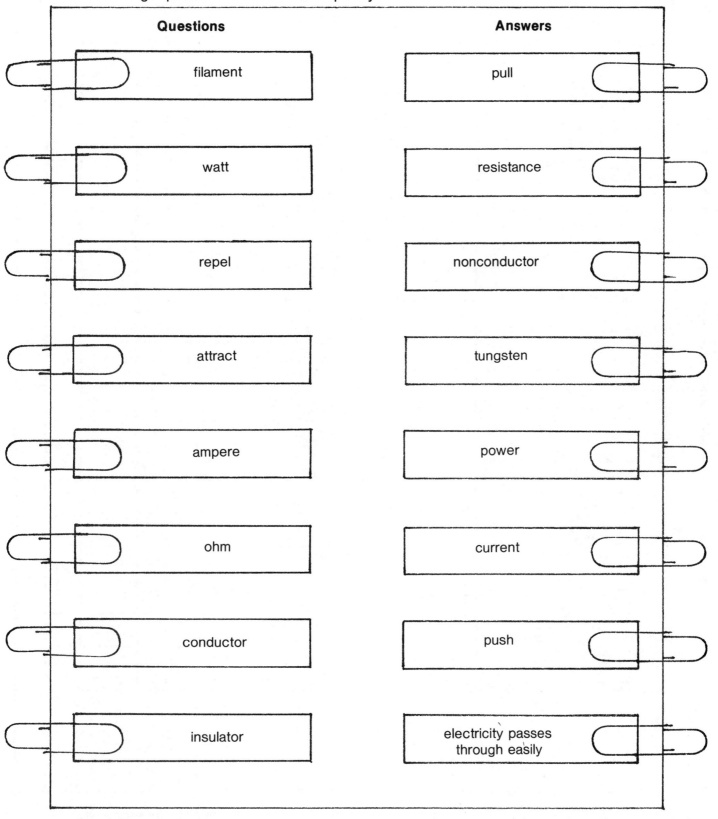

Questions	Answers
filament	pull
watt	resistance
repel	nonconductor
attract	tungsten
ampere	power
ohm	current
conductor	push
insulator	electricity passes through easily

23

PROCESS SKILL(S): RECORD

ELECTRICITY: STUDENT SCHOOL RECORD BOOK

With help from my teacher, I have completed the following electrical activities in school and know how to do the (✔) skills below.

ACTIVITY	DATE	(✔)	ACTIVITY	DATE	(✔)
CHECK (page 2)			COMPARE (page 14)		
*Use a dictionary			*Compare open and closed circuits		
*Define electrical terms			*Identify complete and short circuits		
*Use an encyclopedia			*Compare series and parallel circuits		
*Identify scientists and their discoveries			*Differentiate between incandescent and fluorescent bulbs		
THINK AND REMEMBER (page 4)			ESTIMATE (page 16)		
*Match electrical symbol to object			*Estimate number, size and value of school electrical items		
*Play Concentration			*Appraise the value of electrical objects found in school		
QUESTION (page 6)			MEASURE (page 18)		
*Infer closed electrical circuit			*Measure various lengths of wire		
*Construct black box electrical circuit			*Recognize electrical appliances		
OBSERVE (page 8)			GRAPH (page 20)		
*Discover parts of dry cell			*Identify objects that require DC or AC current		
*Label parts of dry cell			*Show numbers of objects operated on both AC and DC currents		
*Identify parts of light bulb			TEST (page 22)		
*Distinguish parts of light bulb			*Construct bulb holder		
PREDICT (page 10)			*Test closed electrical circuit with bulb holder		
*Compare open and closed circuits			*Construct closed electrical circuit with paper clip switch		
*Identify two points where metal must touch bulb in closed circuit			*Construct quiz game		
*Predict intensity of light bulb using two dry cells			RECORD (page 24)		
*Compute test results			*Keep a record of my school activities in electricity in this book		
CLASSIFY (page 12)			*Record my signature on this record form		
*Discriminate between magnetic and nonmagnetic objects			*Obtain teacher's signature on this record form		
*Test objects for magnetic properties					
*Classify objects as magnetic or nonmagnetic					

My Signature _____   Teacher's Signature _____

24

ELECTRICITY: STUDENT HOME RECORD BOOK

With help from my teacher, I have completed the following electrical activities at home and know how to do the ($\checkmark$) skills below.

ACTIVITY	DATE	($\checkmark$)	ACTIVITY	DATE	($\checkmark$)
CHECK (page 3)			ESTIMATE (page 17)		
*Assess outdoor electrical safety			*Determine the number, size and value of electrical items found around the home		
*Evaluate indoor electrical safety			*Estimate and assess the value of electrical objects in the home		
*Identify and be responsible for obtaining materials for study of electricity			MEASURE (page 19)		
THINK AND REMEMBER (page 5)			*Design electrical wiring of house		
*Draw electrical symbols			*Show how electricity travels in a home		
*Identify electrical objects			GRAPH (page 21)		
QUESTION (page 7)			*Read electric meter		
*Analyze parts of flashlight			*Compute electrical usage		
*Synthesize flashlight parts into workable unit			*Graphically show amount of daily electrical use		
OBSERVE (page 9)			TEST (page 23)		
*Analyze parts of flashlight			*Construct quiz game		
*Reconstruct flashlight			*Test knowledge of electricity		
*Construct intensity device			RECORD (page 25)		
*Conclude path of electricity in flashlight			*Keep a record of my home activities in electricity in this book		
PREDICT (page 11)			*Record my signature on this record form		
*Deduce that unlike magnetic poles attract, like poles repel			*Obtain my parents' signature on this record form		
*Illustrate path of lines of force between two magnets					
CLASSIFY (page 13)					
*Construct conductor tester					
*Distinguish difference between conductors and nonconductors (insulators)					
COMPARE (page 15)					
*Compare static and current electricity					
*Discover electromagnet					
*Compare motor to generator					
*Recognize difference between dry cell and wet cell					

My Signature _____   Parents' Signature _____

25

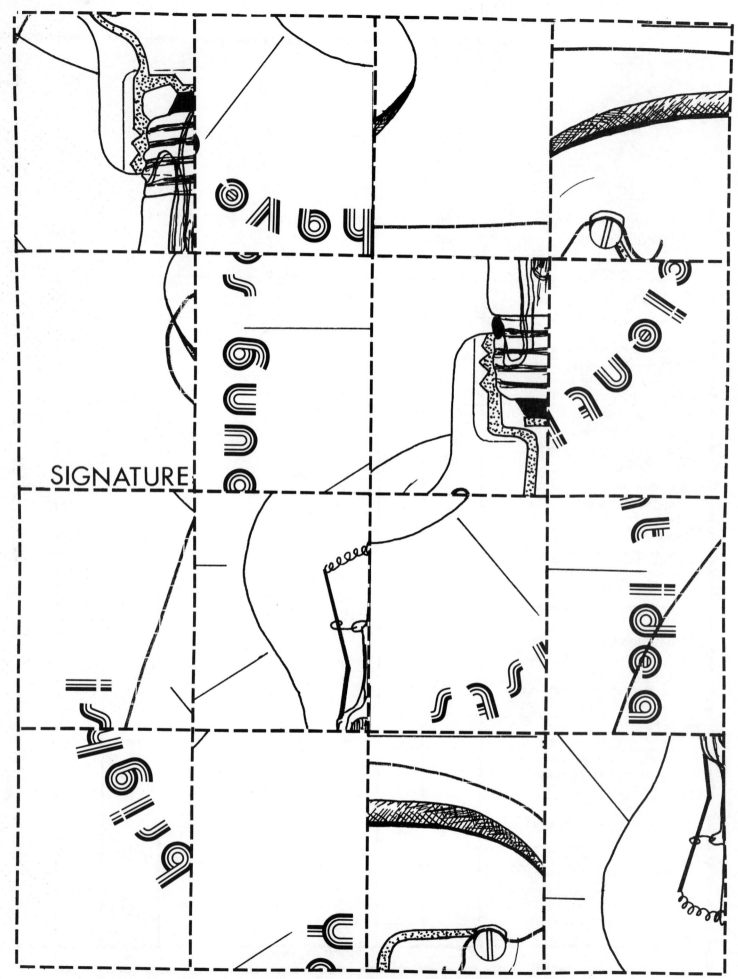

SIGNATURE

TEACHER/PARENT GUIDE

SCIENTISTS DEVELOP PROCESS SKILLS

Activity Page Number ii

Process Skill: Scientific Skills

Concept: Knowledge of the processes of science

Materials: Pencils, one activity page per student

Description: This word search helps youngsters gain an understanding of scientific process skills. Youngsters find, then circle the word for each process skill. Discuss meanings of skills. Have youngsters dramatize each process skill to members of the class. Students identify process skill. Give examples of each. For example, have youngsters estimate the length of their desks to introduce scientific process skill "estimate." Then measure the desk to learn the accuracy of the estimate. Encourage youngsters to use scientific process skills often in their everyday lives.

Answers: Correct answer page looks like this:

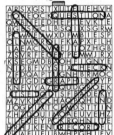

YOUNG SCIENTISTS EXPLORE ELECTRICITY
(front cover)

Activity Page Number 1

Process Skill: General Inquiry

Concept: Career awareness, knowledge of electricity, development of self-concept

Materials: Scissors, glue, stiff cardboard (8½"x11" cardboard from back of writing tablets) or tagboard, laminating machine if available, reference materials

Description: Have youngsters cut activity sheet into designated 16 squares. Rearrange puzzle pieces to make complete picture. Glue pieces in place onto cardboard or tagboard. Add names of student and school. Color. Decorate. Use as front cover for Student's Book. Introduce activity sheet. Show youngsters a cut away dry cell as shown on front cover. Discuss how dry cells are used to power flashlights, electronic toys and games. Note symbols on cover. Youngsters may already know + and − from math class. Discuss qualifications needed to become an electrician. Duplicate back cover of Student Book (activity page 26). Follow same procedure. Laminate both covers. Tape front cover to back cover and use as a folder for pages that make a complete Student Book. Youngsters can also use a manila file folder or a 3-ring binder for this purpose.

Answers: Completed front cover looks like this:

ELECTRICITY REFERENCE MATERIALS

Activity Page Number 2

Process Skill: Check

Concept: Historical events in electricity, electrical terminology

Materials: Pens, pencils, dictionaries, thesaurus, encyclopedia, almanacs, one activity page per student

Description: This activity encourages youngsters to read, alphabetize and define words related to electricity. Directing youngsters to consult an encyclopedia for historical information on electricity is also included. Flip classroom light switch to introduce activity sheet. Ask youngsters to find a word on the dictionary page that describes the object used to turn the lights off and on (switch). Youngsters consult dictionary and define word *switch*. On a separate paper, youngsters write words in alphabetical order and define each. Introduce "B" encyclopedia. Find information on Alexdander Graham Bell who discovered the electric telephone. Youngsters note life span and date of discovery. Match number on page 2 with discovery on page 3. Encourage youngsters to master one term and historical event per day. Develop individual or class dictionaries and encyclopedias of electrical information.

Answers: Ampere, Armature, Atom, Circuit, Compass, Conductor, Copper, Current, Dry Cell, Electrolyte, Electromagnet, Electron, Electroscope, Filament, Generator, Insulator, Magnet, Magnetism, Motor, Ohm, Outlet, Parallel Circuit, Resistance, Series Circuit, Socket, Solenoid, Switch, Transformer, Tungsten, Volt, Voltmeter, Watt, Zinc

14 Tungsten filament, 1 Earth is a huge magnet, 12 Sound recording, 10 Telegraph, 6 Solenoid, 3 Lightning rod, 9 Insulated wire in magnetic coil, 2 X-rays, 4 Generates electricity as current, 13 Wireless telegraphy, 11 Electric telephone, 7 Dynamo, 5 Electric current has a magnetic field, 8 Ohm's Law: Current, voltage, resistance

HOME/SCHOOL SAFETY AND MATERIALS CHECK

Activity Page Number 3

Process Skill: Check

Concept: Electrical safety, identification of electrical materials for study

Materials: Pencils, listed materials at bottom of page, one activity page per student

Description: To introduce lesson, show youngsters the correct way to remove a plug from a wal receptacle (pull plug, not cord). Discuss other electrical safety practices. Give each youngster activity sheet. Identify materials listed at bottom of page that are needed for activities. Teachers may wish to send a letter home asking parents to help child acquire such materials, many of which are found around the home.

Answers: Outdoor Safety 1. ✔, 2. ✔, 3. x, 4. ✔, 5. ✔, 6. x, 7. ✔, 8. ✔, 9. x, 10. ✔, 11. ✔, 12. x, 13. ✔, 14. ✔ Indoor Safety 1. ✔, 2. x, 3. ✔, 4. ✔, 5. ✔, 6. ✔, 7. ✔, 8. ✔, 9. ✔, 10. x, 11. ✔, 12. ✔, 13. x, 14. x

SECRET SYMBOLS CONCENTRATION

Activity Page Number 4

Process Skill: Think, Remember

Concept: Electrical symbols

Materials: Pencils, scissors, glue, cardboard, laminating machine if available, one activity sheet per student.

Description: Youngsters learn how scientists use symbols to represent objects in this activity. Give each youngster one activity sheet. Have youngsters cut apart cards. Glue to cardboard. Make two decks of cards. From the list of words, youngsters print names of objects and matching symbols on cards. Laminate if possible. Play Concentration.

Answers:
(A) = dry cell matched with (G) dry cell
(B) = bulb matched with (H) bulb
(C) = switch matched with (I) switch
(D) = connected wires matched with (J) connected wires
(E) = fuse matched with (K) fuse
(F) = ground matched with (L) ground

SECRET SYMBOLS AROUND HOME

Activity Page Number 5

Process Skill: Think, Remember

Concept: Electrical symbols, electrical objects

Materials: Pencils, reference materials, one activity sheet per student

Description: Encourage youngsters to look for and identify various electrical objects on the page. The names of electrical devices are printed in the blanks next to the boxes. Youngsters should draw matching symbol in appropriate box. Explain role of Underwriter's Laboratory in the promotion of safe electrical equipment. In the scene, the UL symbol is found on the tag attached to the cord of the iron.

Answers:

Picture of Object	Symbol	Name for Symbol
(1) Dry Cells in Flashlight		Dry Cell
(2) Fuse Box or Circuit Breaker		Fuse
(3) Connected Plug Wires		Connected Wires
(4) Iron with UL Safety Tag	U L	Underwriter's Laboratory
(5) Switch		Switch
(6) Microwave cord with ground plug		Ground
(7) Lamp with Bulb		Light Bulb

WHAT'S INSIDE THE BLACK BOX?

Activity Page Number 6

Process Skill: Question

Concept: Closed electrical circuit

Materials: Pencils, cardboard boxes, light bulbs, wires, dry cells, one activity page per student

Description: To introduce activity, show youngsters lighted light bulb protruding from black cardboard box. Brainstorm what may be inside the box that causes the bulb to light. Accept all responses. Use all senses, however, to approve or disapprove ideas. Give youngsters activity sheet. Youngsters "x" boxes of those that cause bulb to light. Discuss each situation: situation 1 is the most possible to occur, situations 2, 3

and 4 are least possible but certainly ideas to consider. Youngsters draw what they think is inside the box at the bottom of page. Be sure youngsters draw a complete circuit if dry cells and wire are used to make bulb light. Distribute equipment. Have youngsters build their own mystery boxes that feature closed electrical circuits.

Answers: Completed project with lighted light bulb.

WHAT'S INSIDE A FLASHLIGHT?

Activity Page Number 7

Process Skill: Question

Concept: Closed electrical circuit in flashlight

Materials: Pencils, scissors, tape, glue, flashlight, one activity page per student

Description: Turn flashlight on and off to introduce activity. Discuss what is in the flashlight that causes bulb to light. Unscrew end of flashlight. Remove dry cells and bulb. Identify each. Give youngsters activity page. Have youngsters cut out parts of flashlight and tape or glue to proper location. Discuss function of leaf spring attached to switch. Develop flashlight display that features mystery stories written by the youngsters.

Answers: Correct answer page looks like this:

OBSERVE THE DRY CELL, LIGHT BULB AND . . .

Activity Page Number 8

Process Skill: Observation

Concept: Parts and function of dry cell and light bulb

Materials: Pencils, pliers, carbon-based dry cell, tape, burned out light bulb, paper sack, one activity page per student

Description: Acquire carbon-based dry cell. CAUTION: Do not use nickel cadmium or alkaline dry cell for this demonstration activity. Carefully take apart dry cell. Identify zinc case, electrolyte paste and carbon rod. Discuss how electricity is produced in the dry cell. Youngsters complete upper portion of activity sheet. Encourage youngsters to save burned out incandescent bulbs for second activity. Exercise caution when breaking bulbs in paper sack. Remove parts carefully. Extend activity to include creative dramatics as each youngster pretends he is a light bulb and traces the path of electricity through his body: extended leg and foot (soder), left side of body (lead-in wire), hair (filament), right side of body (lead in wire), other leg and foot (base). CAUTION: Never allow the body to become a path for the electricity.

Answers: Dry Cell: (1) Carbon Rod, (2) Electrolyte Paste, (3) Zinc Can. Light Bulb: (1) filament, (2) Support Wire, (3) Exhaust Tube, (4) Lead-in Wires, (5) Solder, (6) Base

FLASHLIGHT

Activity Page Number 9

Process Skill: Observation

Concept: Light intensity, closed path of electricity through flashlight

Materials: Pencils, workable flashlight, tissue paper, dictionary, one activity page per student

Description: Review activity page 7. Take apart and reassemble flashlight. Identify each part and its function. Note how bulb touches dry cells which in turn touch coiled spring. Note how leaf spring on switch must make contact with side of bulb socket for flashlight to work. Build "intensity meter" by placing tissue paper over lens. Count number of sheets needed to block out all light (opaque), allows light through but cannot see through (transluscent) and allows light through (transparent). With a pen, have youngsters connect arrows on drawing of flashlight to learn path of electricity through flashlight when in "on" position. Emphasize how switch opens and closes the circuit: open circuit, light is off; closed circuit, light is on. Youngsters may then use intensity meter (sheets of tissue paper) to determine relative intensity of light bulbs in series and parallel circuits.

Answers: Completed project with arrows connected.

Question 1: Flashlight will not light.
Question 2: Leaf spring makes contact with bulb socket to complete circuit.

LIGHT UP AND . . .

Activity Page Number 10

Process Skill: Predict

Concept: Open versus closed circuits

Materials: Pencils, dry cell, light bulb, wires, one activity page per student

Description: This activity stresses a basic discovery method used by scientists: predict, try out, and record results. Give youngsters materials. Do first prediction as a class activity. Circle *Will* or *Won't light*. Try out. Record results of prediction. Complete activity sheet. Compute number correct, incorrect and percent correct. Be sure to emphasize that metal must touch the bulb in two places (side and bottom) for bulb to light.

Answers: Will light: A, B, F, H, J, L.
Won't light: C, D, E (depends on type of dry cell), G, I, K.

ATTRACT!

Activity Page Number 11

Process Skill: Predict

Concept: Opposite magnetic poles attract, like poles repel

Materials: Pencils, bar magnets, horseshoe magnet, iron filings, clear sheet of glass or transparency, one activity page per student

Description: Place two bar magnets end to end on overhead projector leaving short distance between each magnet. Place pane of glass or clear transparency film over magnets. Sprinkle iron filings over magnets. Have youngsters sketch lines of force that show how opposite poles attract and like poles repel. Introduce activity sheet. Youngsters predict which magnets at the bottom of page will be attracted to the north and south poles of the horseshoe magnet at the top of the page. Record numbers in prediction boxes. Then trace correct paths through maze to learn if predictions were correct. Record correct answers in answer boxes. Encourage youngsters to write plays or stories on how this force field could influence people.

Answers: Correct answer page looks like this:

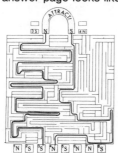

ATTRACTIVE CLASS!

Activity Page Number 12

Process Skill: Classify

Concept: Properties of magnets

Materials: Pencils, magnet, classroom objects, one activity page per student

Description: Introduce activity page by having youngsters predict in the My Guess column whether a paper clip (Magnet—M) and a piece of chalk (Nonmagnet—NM) will be attracted to a magnet. Have a youngster demonstrate how a paper clip is attracted to a magnet and a piece of chalk is not attracted. Place ($\checkmark$) mark in Attracted by Magnet column for paper clip, ($\checkmark$) mark in Not Attracted by Magnet column for the chalk. Complete predictions. Youngsters then circle each hidden object in the puzzle. Have youngsters find these objects in the classroom and test magnetic properties. Complete chart. Check ($\checkmark$) appropriate columns and make a list of other magnetic classroom objects on the chalkboard in the picture.

Answers: Correct answer page looks like this:

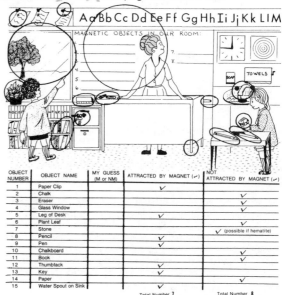

OBJECT NUMBER	OBJECT NAME	MY GUESS (M or NM)	ATTRACTED BY MAGNET ($\checkmark$)	NOT ATTRACTED BY MAGNET ($\checkmark$)
1	Paper Clip		$\checkmark$	
2	Chalk			$\checkmark$
3	Eraser			$\checkmark$
4	Glass Window			$\checkmark$
5	Leg of Desk		$\checkmark$	
6	Plant Leaf			$\checkmark$
7	Stone			$\checkmark$ (possible if hematite)
8	Pencil		$\checkmark$	
9	Pen		$\checkmark$	
10	Chalkboard			$\checkmark$
11	Book			$\checkmark$
12	Thumbtack		$\checkmark$	
13	Key		$\checkmark$	
14	Paper			$\checkmark$
15	Water Spout on Sink		$\checkmark$	
			Total Number 7	Total Number 8

ALL ABOARD: CONDUCTOR CLASSIFICATION

Activity Page Number 13

Process Skill: Classify

Concept: Conductors, nonconductors, and insulators

Materials: Pencils, thumbtacks, wire, dry cell, bulb, empty ball-point pens or wooden meat skewers, various materials such as film can lids, testable objects, one activity page per student

Description: Build and demonstrate a conductor tester. Show youngsters how a paper clip conducts electricity. Construct additional testers. Youngsters test listed materials and classify as good conductors, poor conductors or nonconductors. Point out that a nonconductor is called an insulator.

Answers: Good Conductors—paper clip, silver coin, 5¢ piece, copper cent, aluminum foil
Poor conductors—lead pencil, vinegar, salt water
Nonconductors (Insulators)—wood, glass, plant leaf, leather, rubber, plastic

COMPARISONS AT SCHOOL AND HOME

Activity Page Numbers 14, 15

Process Skill: Compare

Concept(s): Open vs. closed circuits, complete vs. short circuits, static vs. current electricity, series vs. parallel circuits, incandescent vs. fluorescent lights, dry cell vs. wet cell, conductors vs. nonconductors (insulators), magnetic vs. nonmagnetic, motors vs. generators.

Materials: Pencils, one copy of pages 14 and 15 per student

Description: This two-page activity allows youngsters to apply knowledge gained in school directly to a real-life situation. Extend activity by having youngsters develop a list of additional comparisons found at home or school, for example, light vs. dark and heavy vs. light.

Answers: Page 14 (1) Open, (2) Complete, (3) Current, (4) Open, (5) Series, (6) Parallel, (7) Fluorescent, (8) Dry Cell, (9) Nonconductor (insulator), (10) Series, (11) Nonmagnetic, (12) Generator Page 15 (1) Closed, (2) Short, (3) Static, (4) Closed, (5) Parallel, (6) Series, (7) Incandescent, (8) Wet Cell, (9) Conductor, (10) Parallel, (11) Magnetic, (12) Motor

*Concepts on page 14 are opposite of those found on page 15.

SCHOOL ESTIMATES

Activity Page Number 16

Process Skill: Estimate

Concept: Number, size, and appraised value of electrical objects

Materials: Pencils, variety of materials, one activity page per student

Description: In advance, find out the cost of one month's electricity bill for your school. Give each youngster an activity page. Have youngsters estimate the cost of one month's electricity for the school. Record estimate in My Estimate column. Youngsters hold a contest to see who can guess the actual amount. Tell youngsters actual amount. Youngsters calculate difference between original estimate and actual cost in the Difference column. Award prize to winner. Youngsters then complete remaining items on activity sheet.

Answers: Answers will vary with situation or object chosen.

HOME ESTIMATES

Activity Page Number 17

Process Skill: Estimate

Concept: Number, size and appraised value of electrical objects.

Materials: Pencils, variety of materials, one activity page per student

Description: This activity extends those found on page 16 to the home environment. After youngsters have completed this activity, compare results with those found on page 16.

Answers: Answers will vary with situation or object chosen.

MEASURE UP AND . . .

Activity Page Number 18

Process Skill: Measure

Concept: Electrical wiring of house, identification of electrical objects

Materials: Pencils, rulers, string, one activity page per student

Description: This activity encourages youngsters to measure lengths of electrical wire needed to wire a small model home. Introduce activity. Have youngsters measure the distance between two pieces of masking tape. Round off measurements according to age level of student, younger children to the nearest one-half inch (cm). Give each youngster an activity sheet. With a string or ruler measure distance from A (Transformer) to B (Electric Meter) as large group activity (4.0 inches) (10.0 cm). Round off as needed. Complete page. Emphasize that youngsters will use these actual measurements to trace wires in house circuits on page 19.

Answers: A-B 4.0 in., 10.00 cm; B-C 0.5 in., 1.25 cm; C-D 1.0 in., 2.54 cm; C-E 4.0 in., 10.00 cm; C-F 5.0 in., 12.50 cm; C-G 4.0 in., 10.00 cm; H-E 2.5 in., 6.25 cm; C-I 1.5 in., 3.75 cm; C-J 6.25 in., 15.60 cm; C-K 4.0 in., 10.00 cm; C-L 6.25 in., 15.60 cm; C-M 1.0 in., 2.54 cm

WIRE UP

Activity Page Number 19

Process Skill: Measure

Concept: House wiring, electrical appliances and objects

Materials: Pencils, scissors, colored pens, glue, wire, thin rubber bands, or string (optional), rulers, one activity page per student

Description: Review lengths of wire on page 18. Give youngsters page 19. Have youngsters measure and record lengths of wires on lines drawn at bottom of page. Using a different colored pen for each wire, youngsters trace path of wire to make complete circuit. Extend activity for older youngsters by having them glue fine wire, string, yarn, or thin rubber bands to connect identified points. Youngsters can also use their schematic diagram to wire a home constructed from a cardboard box. Use dry cells, wire and small light bulbs to illuminate each room in the home. Some youngsters may want to add a small radio or other electrical gadget. Encourage the development of a play whose script features a story of the route electricity travels throughout a home.

Answers: See Teacher Guide for page 18.

HELP FIND AC AND DC

Activity Page Number 20

Process Skill: Graphing

Concept: Alternating current, Direct current

Materials: Pencils, crayons, one activity page per student

Description: Introduce activity with a review of objects that operate on alternating (AC) current (60 cycles) versus those that run on direct (DC) current. Make a simple bar graph of such objects found in the classroom. Introduce activity sheet. Youngsters locate AC and DC operated objects, write the names of objects in the blanks and color in the correct number of such objects on the appropriate graphs.

Answers: Correct answer page looks like this:

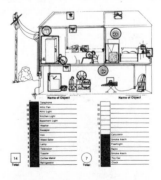